This book belongs to

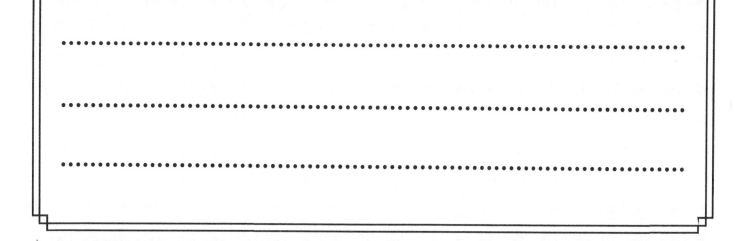

....

....

....

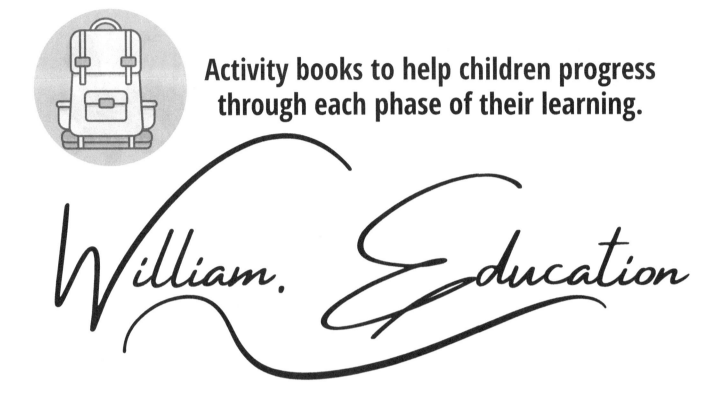

Activity books to help children progress through each phase of their learning.

Don't hesitate to give your opinion (constructive ;-)) and your ideas for improvement after your purchase, because I really want to offer quality activities. Have fun!

Peaperback ASIN : 9798822037663

Math Practice

Addition and Subtraction
Multiplication And Division

William. Education

37 + 78	22 + 85	18 + 71	66 + 45
62 + 23	68 + 36	93 + 42	68 + 90
78 + 91	76 + 76	39 + 67	10 + 89
28 + 42	50 + 27	53 + 22	83 + 75
34 + 72	46 + 30	15 + 87	19 + 27
62 + 21	60 + 79	36 + 74	49 + 62
99 + 20	82 + 76	28 + 71	44 + 86
31 + 20	92 + 54	13 + 44	84 + 95

Notes

 Time: Score: /32

58 + 77	73 + 45	55 + 75	31 + 72
79 + 88	17 + 89	92 + 52	87 + 94
79 + 36	26 + 88	72 + 82	17 + 37
28 + 23	78 + 72	50 + 79	98 + 30
65 + 90	58 + 92	13 + 74	61 + 45
63 + 82	70 + 49	49 + 97	9 + 27
40 + 85	57 + 34	70 + 58	69 + 41
22 + 92	30 + 28	41 + 89	91 + 97

 Time: **Score:**

Double Digit Addition

11 + 79	72 + 74	25 + 94	58 + 25
82 + 55	20 + 76	83 + 97	68 + 34
90 + 40	88 + 62	89 + 79	34 + 71
34 + 47	12 + 96	50 + 77	89 + 41
47 + 54	48 + 78	57 + 42	73 + 94
75 + 85	75 + 44	38 + 86	45 + 19
56 + 88	93 + 89	59 + 68	75 + 83
38 + 61	55 + 69	22 + 48	53 + 22

 Time: Score: /32

Double Digit Addition

98 + 46	41 + 58	21 + 77	77 + 45
56 + 44	18 + 94	51 + 62	16 + 45
54 + 39	48 + 87	30 + 43	16 + 63
48 + 69	18 + 44	94 + 62	41 + 25
93 + 96	54 + 55	50 + 59	32 + 80
95 + 55	33 + 83	60 + 44	84 + 33
66 + 59	17 + 75	90 + 53	14 + 80
58 + 69	34 + 23	95 + 64	55 + 67

 Time: Score: /32

Double Digit Addition

66 + 77	22 + 87	25 + 89	20 + 31
51 + 40	72 + 64	59 + 56	69 + 38
56 + 86	60 + 96	10 + 30	32 + 75
54 + 35	22 + 49	28 + 24	79 + 95
26 + 24	19 + 74	48 + 69	67 + 33
26 + 35	63 + 86	76 + 72	14 + 73
41 + 99	74 + 40	98 + 77	36 + 49
71 + 39	97 + 70	61 + 37	23 + 94

 Time: Score: 32

Double Digit Addition

16 + 79	51 + 96	73 + 74	74 + 37
48 + 83	55 + 99	29 + 21	28 + 93
62 + 50	28 + 48	28 + 89	31 + 92
96 + 30	48 + 85	93 + 36	83 + 60
34 + 94	64 + 78	94 + 41	65 + 67
19 + 65	97 + 70	80 + 37	90 + 25
27 + 80	43 + 57	55 + 71	58 + 56
80 + 71	77 + 47	14 + 81	80 + 42

Notes

Time: Score: /32

Double Digit Addition

70 + 68	68 + 19	79 + 53	79 + 90
61 + 32	61 + 54	72 + 75	10 + 59
67 + 50	99 + 60	85 + 74	43 + 99
52 + 29	37 + 64	61 + 35	22 + 59
64 + 21	96 + 73	55 + 42	21 + 48
41 + 86	91 + 43	95 + 91	42 + 67
49 + 50	22 + 85	13 + 51	38 + 47
47 + 44	67 + 39	54 + 86	89 + 29

Notes
_____

 Time: Score: /32

Double Digit Addition

73 + 53	40 + 48	82 + 96	22 + 43
85 + 48	91 + 83	61 + 84	44 + 31
60 + 83	50 + 21	44 + 76	16 + 20
75 + 77	50 + 52	71 + 48	41 + 87
30 + 97	35 + 50	30 + 75	66 + 45
19 + 57	46 + 19	56 + 70	70 + 77
62 + 71	39 + 73	67 + 63	21 + 24
42 + 20	21 + 19	26 + 50	34 + 78

Notes

 Time: Score: /32

Double Digit Addition

37 + 88	15 + 77	45 + 82	77 + 33
56 + 42	75 + 94	84 + 71	98 + 54
54 + 85	66 + 81	42 + 91	38 + 47
54 + 75	72 + 95	47 + 45	21 + 71
52 + 22	65 + 73	91 + 28	77 + 78
53 + 58	61 + 34	21 + 24	58 + 89
26 + 61	62 + 41	29 + 71	90 + 56
90 + 34	73 + 41	71 + 85	34 + 63

Notes

 Time: **Score:**   **/32**

Double Digit Addition

56 + 31	95 + 78	21 + 91	55 + 83
71 + 97	70 + 41	84 + 31	10 + 59
40 + 41	96 + 52	91 + 59	38 + 76
27 + 29	41 + 31	98 + 31	24 + 19
53 + 76	65 + 82	30 + 58	12 + 92
91 + 35	37 + 44	97 + 36	71 + 61
57 + 59	36 + 69	29 + 98	15 + 49
55 + 68	72 + 67	51 + 55	73 + 21

Notes

 Time: **Score:** /**32**

88 + 82	14 + 25	95 + 56	29 + 67
42 + 68	49 + 34	72 + 22	75 + 33
83 + 91	60 + 30	23 + 27	30 + 54
10 + 57	49 + 34	51 + 94	63 + 89
81 + 25	77 + 86	62 + 92	90 + 41
9 + 21	26 + 34	51 + 81	58 + 95
30 + 28	33 + 44	44 + 29	20 + 97
40 + 20	62 + 37	33 + 58	89 + 82

 Time:

Score: /32

Double Digit Addition

69 + 26	85 + 73	58 + 59	28 + 21
22 + 42	15 + 62	31 + 62	78 + 63
76 + 91	45 + 75	41 + 36	59 + 46
98 + 87	89 + 68	43 + 39	22 + 77
96 + 22	58 + 45	56 + 85	18 + 19
30 + 64	81 + 78	10 + 97	71 + 98
74 + 21	88 + 66	54 + 42	49 + 28
94 + 88	47 + 56	51 + 32	85 + 82

Notes

 Time: Score: /32

Double Digit Addition

14 + 34	19 + 49	68 + 81	78 + 30
94 + 28	84 + 90	14 + 54	91 + 75
28 + 44	88 + 33	48 + 40	91 + 53
25 + 81	16 + 81	72 + 87	41 + 67
73 + 74	69 + 98	18 + 79	40 + 33
98 + 98	48 + 23	41 + 27	25 + 61
19 + 61	63 + 84	59 + 44	20 + 52
17 + 48	96 + 85	68 + 25	31 + 42

 Time:

Score: /32

Double Digit Addition

51 + 23	69 + 40	52 + 36	46 + 21
45 + 66	98 + 29	31 + 42	93 + 67
55 + 78	19 + 21	74 + 47	66 + 78
36 + 66	91 + 82	50 + 39	68 + 38
82 + 21	64 + 73	98 + 23	96 + 45
40 + 37	33 + 32	39 + 76	17 + 22
10 + 20	52 + 33	33 + 85	14 + 81
49 + 96	64 + 68	73 + 41	95 + 91

Notes

Time: Score: /32

Double Digit Addition

71 + 21	67 + 75	13 + 39	74 + 85
95 + 94	15 + 56	11 + 66	29 + 25
28 + 43	97 + 64	80 + 85	63 + 27
20 + 70	83 + 28	22 + 85	64 + 86
53 + 78	80 + 71	36 + 87	81 + 92
45 + 32	93 + 56	95 + 78	98 + 87
31 + 38	97 + 62	40 + 72	48 + 85
60 + 85	81 + 92	10 + 96	23 + 32

Notes

 Time: Score: /32

Double Digit Addition

10 + 84	98 + 38	66 + 48	24 + 88
76 + 66	42 + 90	70 + 84	27 + 23
34 + 58	10 + 48	59 + 41	60 + 47
65 + 36	18 + 47	36 + 51	19 + 51
48 + 33	47 + 25	20 + 53	81 + 19
37 + 61	84 + 35	95 + 35	14 + 44
41 + 95	98 + 29	56 + 53	65 + 60
50 + 71	10 + 42	18 + 47	37 + 54

 Notes _____

 Time: Score: / 32

Double Digit Addition

30 + 23	67 + 56	75 + 54	56 + 61
35 + 22	83 + 91	88 + 86	58 + 25
45 + 19	49 + 61	67 + 97	69 + 97
30 + 71	39 + 62	83 + 70	28 + 85
41 + 86	10 + 30	65 + 88	12 + 20
24 + 30	36 + 44	31 + 23	83 + 86
85 + 37	75 + 68	18 + 48	43 + 25
85 + 46	73 + 90	60 + 54	11 + 87

Notes

 Time:

Score:

 /32

Double Digit Addition

17 + 80	32 + 62	34 + 51	66 + 76
94 + 56	55 + 88	48 + 56	85 + 57
92 + 38	31 + 31	20 + 31	42 + 53
56 + 25	96 + 22	51 + 21	74 + 30
50 + 28	73 + 85	16 + 77	65 + 44
22 + 52	87 + 82	86 + 93	83 + 79
25 + 58	44 + 23	78 + 25	71 + 78
41 + 45	21 + 90	35 + 41	20 + 39

Notes

 Time: Score: /32

95 + 41	87 + 20	43 + 60	91 + 45
94 + 85	15 + 41	88 + 39	65 + 90
90 + 89	73 + 80	74 + 83	56 + 78
90 + 52	77 + 58	88 + 22	28 + 68
57 + 30	92 + 64	17 + 95	69 + 74
76 + 58	19 + 90	97 + 90	20 + 23
65 + 94	83 + 47	25 + 20	66 + 94
45 + 93	30 + 29	11 + 20	24 + 59

_____
_____
_____
_____
_____

 Time: Score: /32

Double Digit Addition

63 + 32	64 + 86	30 + 48	89 + 31
87 + 84	10 + 22	99 + 67	97 + 97
92 + 70	88 + 68	71 + 52	93 + 63
45 + 97	25 + 26	14 + 31	56 + 92
98 + 62	86 + 64	35 + 98	54 + 63
61 + 31	70 + 58	48 + 48	87 + 42
86 + 41	45 + 82	56 + 19	43 + 77
65 + 30	89 + 62	68 + 69	39 + 71

Notes _____

 Time: **Score:**   /**32**

Triple Digit Addition

730 + 239	933 + 546	617 + 178	867 + 433
881 + 433	150 + 994	557 + 787	894 + 355
183 + 235	823 + 450	794 + 116	350 + 466
940 + 631	331 + 858	434 + 939	872 + 830
691 + 335	304 + 321	768 + 484	228 + 129
381 + 956	798 + 723	453 + 387	298 + 624
398 + 744	908 + 386	552 + 401	816 + 143
218 + 106	382 + 542	276 + 731	288 + 607

Notes

_____

_____

_____

_____

_____

 Time:

Score:

 /32

264 + 920	123 + 444	192 + 907	680 + 721
748 + 753	503 + 408	874 + 167	124 + 372
354 + 223	454 + 596	818 + 779	304 + 624
957 + 441	174 + 997	852 + 288	622 + 348
462 + 346	327 + 405	675 + 183	138 + 866
712 + 788	984 + 778	764 + 583	861 + 178
647 + 667	835 + 836	512 + 371	476 + 278
509 + 639	130 + 514	513 + 909	661 + 478

Notes

 Time:

Score: /**32**

203 + 587	551 + 306	179 + 310	185 + 474
345 + 127	665 + 925	593 + 426	985 + 753
426 + 908	716 + 561	343 + 560	310 + 123
992 + 580	632 + 227	499 + 521	269 + 954
162 + 245	137 + 675	222 + 185	275 + 595
267 + 382	387 + 167	295 + 748	723 + 998
535 + 636	906 + 516	260 + 349	371 + 112
911 + 201	960 + 823	235 + 418	804 + 749

Notes _____

_____

_____

_____

_____

 **Time:**   **Score:**   **32**

Triple Digit Addition

658 + 631	429 + 312	395 + 606	794 + 130
635 + 954	931 + 240	465 + 158	999 + 718
927 + 722	809 + 512	786 + 651	453 + 426
238 + 429	784 + 132	517 + 410	133 + 282
406 + 506	233 + 450	765 + 823	164 + 452
817 + 307	533 + 881	989 + 538	152 + 451
467 + 474	189 + 453	444 + 583	502 + 766
464 + 846	184 + 957	543 + 992	988 + 287

Notes

Time: Score: /32

275 + 989	489 + 951	680 + 395	444 + 297
860 + 538	390 + 132	579 + 104	953 + 653
680 + 777	187 + 120	786 + 268	147 + 547
904 + 134	656 + 143	160 + 992	369 + 142
837 + 148	773 + 829	132 + 881	475 + 303
419 + 926	103 + 739	101 + 503	269 + 486
446 + 734	784 + 883	989 + 693	100 + 889
629 + 226	912 + 295	824 + 614	591 + 632

Notes

 Time:

Score: /32

Triple Digit Addition

418 + 433	998 + 514	986 + 149	947 + 537
775 + 753	750 + 391	190 + 117	833 + 801
633 + 507	471 + 704	307 + 779	400 + 662
587 + 716	882 + 345	553 + 776	248 + 106
121 + 751	460 + 349	926 + 310	715 + 539
508 + 738	968 + 794	111 + 749	554 + 346
373 + 901	681 + 451	751 + 906	294 + 341
537 + 102	996 + 124	814 + 186	699 + 423

Notes
_____
_____
_____
_____
_____

 Time: **Score:**   **/32**

640 + 130	826 + 253	489 + 566	881 + 820
271 + 981	611 + 723	558 + 931	235 + 377
450 + 390	114 + 921	892 + 712	522 + 275
763 + 753	172 + 404	184 + 603	360 + 239
160 + 158	944 + 747	423 + 679	329 + 728
807 + 796	466 + 832	912 + 349	349 + 903
150 + 317	412 + 125	531 + 408	352 + 840
660 + 927	998 + 457	367 + 242	328 + 675

Notes

 Time:　　　　**Score:**　　 **/32**

552 + 452	367 + 595	499 + 144	717 + 803
198 + 722	370 + 246	885 + 938	456 + 477
162 + 605	803 + 656	626 + 140	841 + 698
615 + 523	943 + 668	888 + 271	757 + 914
249 + 221	766 + 107	291 + 199	266 + 304
108 + 590	745 + 510	612 + 321	793 + 436
404 + 239	625 + 407	805 + 348	277 + 437
445 + 130	505 + 871	120 + 370	207 + 868

 Time: **Score:**   /**32**

641 + 327	265 + 592	340 + 160	737 + 528
652 + 939	505 + 943	763 + 339	550 + 590
170 + 399	619 + 222	117 + 126	142 + 931
629 + 450	337 + 838	146 + 353	446 + 815
256 + 944	474 + 435	894 + 348	623 + 936
496 + 918	524 + 701	948 + 875	542 + 649
167 + 523	368 + 845	359 + 558	482 + 135
367 + 486	440 + 692	620 + 514	694 + 987

 Time: Score: /32

382 + 240	317 + 498	513 + 503	391 + 766
103 + 434	127 + 277	420 + 170	146 + 524
633 + 933	895 + 352	639 + 517	285 + 930
893 + 297	297 + 283	126 + 515	367 + 566
908 + 324	942 + 931	954 + 441	651 + 843
418 + 849	254 + 904	427 + 991	338 + 692
780 + 994	471 + 993	223 + 278	166 + 813
402 + 291	649 + 365	752 + 765	548 + 870

Notes

Time: **Score:**   **/32**

772 + 734	906 + 815	402 + 294	550 + 99
697 + 912	367 + 235	138 + 762	621 + 864
329 + 537	504 + 753	971 + 134	680 + 162
494 + 292	732 + 211	785 + 126	226 + 115
912 + 798	619 + 634	623 + 329	250 + 360
265 + 919	940 + 451	179 + 398	387 + 534
423 + 450	686 + 589	691 + 942	652 + 649
972 + 236	883 + 260	194 + 759	186 + 501

Notes _____
_____
_____
_____
_____
_____

 Time: Score: /32

407 + 508	849 + 377	924 + 972	235 + 410
716 + 422	406 + 582	143 + 557	930 + 511
499 + 347	587 + 202	591 + 171	758 + 945
679 + 113	781 + 441	334 + 313	471 + 642
972 + 793	544 + 153	248 + 866	764 + 456
605 + 937	126 + 728	933 + 719	396 + 316
671 + 905	881 + 496	724 + 251	210 + 117
100 + 681	134 + 566	593 + 615	868 + 698

 Time: **Score:** **/32**

728 + 143	736 + 103	101 + 560	870 + 645
986 + 703	941 + 571	882 + 570	190 + 804
990 + 467	760 + 249	592 + 410	640 + 980
168 + 526	193 + 476	694 + 506	418 + 818
938 + 422	631 + 492	973 + 262	136 + 258
690 + 313	314 + 715	698 + 466	966 + 931
684 + 402	745 + 521	419 + 216	197 + 878
619 + 563	651 + 293	175 + 825	733 + 337

 Time: Score:

Triple Digit Addition

139 + 449	469 + 793	442 + 765	973 + 112
905 + 698	712 + 276	256 + 334	881 + 222
605 + 667	282 + 346	130 + 143	543 + 861
971 + 928	552 + 591	291 + 842	495 + 749
982 + 414	717 + 407	418 + 508	118 + 344
837 + 183	105 + 697	638 + 833	624 + 325
157 + 727	173 + 653	426 + 708	794 + 407
247 + 206	463 + 991	604 + 166	239 + 352

Notes

Time:

Score:

 /32

189 + 381	314 + 351	787 + 930	943 + 992
839 + 120	732 + 766	411 + 404	663 + 749
367 + 652	169 + 202	253 + 256	266 + 493
751 + 926	525 + 231	174 + 334	477 + 660
386 + 466	344 + 618	225 + 824	235 + 285
299 + 808	895 + 293	111 + 609	487 + 775
875 + 187	107 + 442	608 + 102	241 + 800
286 + 980	493 + 468	460 + 531	420 + 234

Notes _____

_____

_____

_____

_____

 Time: **Score:**   **/32**

260 + 702	142 + 725	408 + 880	646 + 124
653 + 835	950 + 122	982 + 625	743 + 930
896 + 881	904 + 120	359 + 711	708 + 217
973 + 800	375 + 123	901 + 482	349 + 374
959 + 820	733 + 426	956 + 341	521 + 170
602 + 278	343 + 512	926 + 567	713 + 461
606 + 574	792 + 931	652 + 419	500 + 909
953 + 659	108 + 963	174 + 281	234 + 454

Notes

_____

_____

_____

_____

 Time: Score: /32

375 + 347	259 + 347	791 + 908	354 + 897
138 + 312	445 + 911	274 + 284	714 + 632
497 + 952	903 + 134	776 + 706	363 + 288
355 + 593	733 + 713	724 + 269	326 + 179
641 + 668	319 + 454	625 + 327	663 + 940
249 + 635	659 + 336	841 + 311	637 + 130
419 + 651	704 + 273	524 + 893	554 + 726
570 + 718	145 + 611	756 + 390	403 + 379

 Time: Score: /32

Triple Digit Addition

668 + 921	410 + 700	545 + 175	461 + 221
962 + 507	283 + 303	943 + 210	117 + 635
710 + 764	817 + 788	482 + 453	900 + 809
863 + 833	634 + 495	388 + 943	174 + 257
891 + 830	523 + 876	674 + 923	834 + 816
890 + 808	515 + 945	696 + 254	230 + 615
374 + 533	847 + 976	154 + 659	278 + 588
443 + 489	895 + 720	687 + 366	614 + 630

Notes

Time: **Score:**   /**32**

Double Digit Subtraction

91 − 74	64 − 62	55 − 15	64 − 40
82 − 71	91 − 31	88 − 80	85 − 29
50 − 48	82 − 76	63 − 61	84 − 58
98 − 55	88 − 76	82 − 39	84 − 31
59 − 38	79 − 35	46 − 20	87 − 77
93 − 62	39 − 16	53 − 40	76 − 53
89 − 26	88 − 74	41 − 22	66 − 47
62 − 18	66 − 64	93 − 51	76 − 32

 Time: Score: /32

Triple Digit Addition

824 + 413	265 + 430	531 + 712	267 + 379
541 + 329	596 + 113	730 + 635	292 + 384
459 + 530	121 + 922	648 + 420	730 + 264
268 + 220	330 + 202	453 + 823	141 + 365
600 + 418	544 + 984	389 + 552	161 + 150
197 + 778	199 + 971	670 + 647	908 + 589
548 + 837	945 + 516	663 + 488	858 + 663
509 + 689	938 + 806	460 + 222	975 + 671

Notes

Time:

Score:

 /32

Double Digit Subtraction

90 − 40	57 − 49	77 − 74	93 − 75
87 − 82	93 − 70	76 − 50	41 − 24
48 − 22	95 − 39	48 − 43	59 − 47
82 − 63	42 − 13	41 − 27	60 − 44
85 − 78	91 − 81	98 − 84	72 − 10
93 − 23	67 − 51	56 − 10	99 − 23
67 − 60	95 − 69	39 − 23	41 − 41
74 − 70	65 − 49	94 − 16	76 − 36

Notes

 Time:

Score: /32

Double Digit Subtraction

56 - 47	79 - 60	71 - 64	90 - 76
68 - 23	97 - 26	68 - 66	64 - 23
34 - 27	83 - 32	84 - 69	67 - 33
54 - 48	98 - 58	98 - 50	99 - 97
91 - 28	82 - 40	64 - 55	67 - 33
55 - 9	49 - 15	31 - 19	72 - 23
85 - 65	74 - 59	91 - 52	62 - 42
97 - 44	79 - 28	85 - 40	72 - 62

 Time: Score: /32

Double Digit Subtraction

96 - 58	39 - 26	66 - 45	67 - 12
45 - 24	97 - 61	99 - 19	94 - 66
88 - 41	21 - 20	83 - 47	39 - 36
92 - 26	58 - 47	92 - 46	35 - 9
86 - 16	86 - 21	97 - 40	79 - 11
89 - 81	67 - 59	89 - 76	92 - 66
69 - 18	79 - 61	76 - 33	48 - 32
84 - 10	73 - 68	76 - 42	87 - 21

 Notes _____

_____

_____

_____

_____

 Time: Score: /32

Double Digit Subtraction

72 - 38	76 - 39	40 - 24	65 - 36
79 - 28	81 - 23	46 - 43	95 - 68
40 - 23	33 - 23	54 - 13	77 - 22
51 - 50	72 - 50	95 - 12	88 - 41
66 - 47	86 - 40	31 - 24	47 - 30
85 - 59	57 - 38	94 - 71	70 - 55
94 - 49	98 - 95	62 - 44	53 - 38
94 - 9	84 - 77	94 - 29	47 - 41

Notes

Time: **Score:**   /32

Double Digit Subtraction

76 − 47	43 − 25	84 − 42	74 − 61
32 − 21	98 − 25	73 − 31	49 − 49
29 − 16	83 − 75	55 − 17	85 − 57
72 − 28	95 − 25	70 − 55	52 − 51
63 − 27	52 − 28	98 − 68	53 − 39
88 − 39	58 − 34	41 − 13	54 − 43
75 − 22	88 − 78	96 − 18	94 − 26
78 − 63	94 − 21	89 − 45	67 − 22

 **Time:** **Score:** **/32**

89 - 74	82 - 46	91 - 66	21 - 9
76 - 27	63 - 23	57 - 34	24 - 15
67 - 45	38 - 22	94 - 13	94 - 74
76 - 53	71 - 30	87 - 31	78 - 59
79 - 77	34 - 29	37 - 35	76 - 44
96 - 19	95 - 33	55 - 12	79 - 38
94 - 47	74 - 35	53 - 20	92 - 34
91 - 59	80 - 37	42 - 13	51 - 35

 Time: **Score:**   **32**

Double Digit Subtraction

87 - 10	23 - 22	80 - 79	29 - 24
89 - 58	87 - 61	72 - 22	69 - 60
74 - 35	95 - 66	96 - 55	24 - 16
62 - 55	57 - 19	87 - 83	92 - 74
60 - 46	37 - 34	61 - 52	96 - 35
61 - 49	84 - 59	53 - 52	66 - 35
84 - 75	84 - 9	61 - 10	80 - 72
97 - 24	78 - 39	86 - 34	78 - 44

 **Time:** **Score:** /**32**

Double Digit Subtraction

40 - 19	73 - 21	92 - 80	58 - 37
90 - 41	25 - 20	66 - 63	87 - 64
82 - 43	52 - 28	80 - 27	96 - 80
46 - 37	76 - 39	82 - 45	63 - 33
64 - 28	94 - 56	52 - 44	69 - 24
41 - 27	72 - 39	83 - 40	76 - 17
75 - 53	84 - 44	41 - 22	44 - 28
73 - 27	80 - 26	52 - 46	76 - 25

 Notes

 Time: Score: /32

Double Digit Subtraction

61 - 20	97 - 46	87 - 60	89 - 27
69 - 17	59 - 20	93 - 81	88 - 68
99 - 93	41 - 21	97 - 11	47 - 34
64 - 30	92 - 20	77 - 42	90 - 41
81 - 55	92 - 75	73 - 12	52 - 46
69 - 21	30 - 15	99 - 72	62 - 45
82 - 75	73 - 55	70 - 64	85 - 64
72 - 65	76 - 57	52 - 26	46 - 27

_____

_____

_____

_____

_____

 Time:

Score: /32

Double Digit Subtraction

56 - 53	52 - 48	78 - 36	60 - 48
55 - 35	62 - 19	67 - 19	93 - 58
95 - 46	80 - 64	71 - 56	40 - 22
69 - 29	63 - 45	85 - 41	45 - 16
44 - 15	93 - 74	87 - 26	49 - 31
48 - 30	84 - 20	98 - 64	91 - 43
53 - 20	90 - 82	83 - 67	38 - 27
84 - 16	75 - 70	81 - 30	32 - 22

Notes

 Time: **Score:** **/32**

Double Digit Subtraction

97 - 28	24 - 19	96 - 86	89 - 28
58 - 28	46 - 26	70 - 48	66 - 60
55 - 55	96 - 26	32 - 15	60 - 28
71 - 50	86 - 37	65 - 25	91 - 91
54 - 28	96 - 67	85 - 33	53 - 52
56 - 38	79 - 52	73 - 61	91 - 66
98 - 36	22 - 13	75 - 63	90 - 69
78 - 25	80 - 51	84 - 46	90 - 30

 Time: **Score:**   **/32**

Double Digit Subtraction

66 − 54	88 − 86	64 − 54	96 − 63
55 − 32	75 − 23	32 − 21	91 − 29
72 − 70	89 − 82	80 − 48	73 − 71
59 − 20	96 − 87	76 − 29	74 − 69
42 − 25	90 − 83	86 − 27	84 − 46
96 − 63	61 − 52	55 − 42	85 − 77
54 − 27	82 − 27	46 − 28	42 − 20
71 − 54	90 − 73	58 − 54	78 − 12

Notes

Time: Score: /32

Double Digit Subtraction

80 - 52	59 - 56	86 - 62	60 - 16
85 - 11	41 - 23	98 - 56	74 - 64
20 - 16	48 - 36	43 - 36	65 - 15
37 - 23	76 - 47	73 - 56	66 - 39
38 - 16	67 - 63	94 - 32	80 - 27
80 - 34	95 - 19	51 - 48	51 - 17
68 - 28	75 - 72	65 - 20	91 - 56
88 - 24	70 - 34	96 - 43	47 - 42

 Time:

Score: /32

38 - 23	84 - 83	90 - 83	82 - 44
87 - 56	89 - 15	96 - 73	96 - 27
59 - 51	91 - 30	94 - 78	97 - 79
30 - 22	89 - 13	77 - 52	95 - 22
89 - 42	64 - 43	92 - 31	55 - 36
95 - 40	52 - 36	63 - 30	57 - 50
63 - 27	57 - 55	99 - 72	66 - 29
90 - 39	91 - 23	93 - 89	68 - 41

Notes _____

 Time:

Score:

 /32

38 - 33	95 - 76	60 - 59	44 - 26
42 - 42	96 - 94	68 - 27	34 - 29
29 - 28	88 - 67	81 - 46	78 - 29
77 - 31	94 - 79	74 - 25	39 - 21
31 - 11	89 - 68	80 - 54	62 - 43
89 - 44	48 - 18	81 - 76	57 - 18
74 - 44	36 - 31	38 - 37	78 - 39
88 - 47	87 - 35	43 - 33	89 - 45

 Time: 　　　　Score: /32

Double Digit Subtraction

61 - 15	89 - 25	53 - 33	64 - 19
76 - 20	93 - 39	77 - 63	54 - 39
92 - 22	95 - 82	68 - 64	90 - 63
53 - 51	56 - 51	78 - 35	69 - 35
93 - 91	77 - 54	49 - 22	86 - 52
96 - 87	96 - 80	71 - 13	81 - 57
83 - 46	87 - 72	77 - 15	98 - 35
66 - 38	80 - 24	69 - 30	83 - 82

Notes _____

_____

_____

_____

_____

 Time: **Score:**   **/32**

56 - 28	89 - 46	94 - 57	78 - 12
76 - 12	96 - 40	58 - 18	55 - 25
95 - 33	74 - 25	73 - 34	55 - 34
94 - 11	95 - 94	64 - 22	92 - 21
58 - 26	93 - 64	22 - 22	96 - 29
55 - 16	76 - 66	69 - 31	48 - 16
46 - 27	90 - 43	99 - 82	81 - 27
74 - 29	86 - 81	72 - 63	93 - 88

Notes

 Time: Score: /32

Double Digit Subtraction

77 - 23	92 - 45	75 - 23	53 - 50
91 - 47	59 - 28	95 - 29	56 - 16
68 - 64	85 - 85	91 - 35	57 - 46
87 - 67	98 - 75	74 - 71	70 - 59
30 - 10	93 - 83	80 - 69	88 - 24
89 - 24	94 - 17	55 - 28	91 - 37
55 - 32	95 - 28	71 - 56	76 - 51
80 - 62	64 - 60	45 - 29	66 - 55

 Notes _____

_____

_____

_____

_____

_____

 Time: Score: /32

Triple Digit Subtraction

561 - 124	367 - 199	734 - 237	973 - 933
627 - 509	787 - 296	989 - 516	313 - 303
515 - 127	847 - 149	973 - 819	651 - 483
854 - 392	809 - 375	953 - 385	761 - 152
751 - 161	655 - 343	480 - 106	520 - 230
507 - 339	670 - 489	925 - 427	274 - 212
899 - 344	311 - 293	631 - 507	973 - 842
853 - 667	943 - 505	763 - 207	590 - 386

 Time: Score: /32

Double Digit Subtraction

88 - 83	91 - 90	73 - 61	72 - 23
96 - 82	96 - 66	98 - 92	58 - 22
80 - 50	77 - 51	94 - 54	66 - 42
32 - 10	78 - 77	95 - 56	94 - 29
90 - 17	40 - 35	57 - 17	76 - 17
46 - 28	78 - 51	72 - 40	90 - 78
99 - 43	87 - 52	86 - 46	55 - 31
83 - 40	81 - 45	84 - 66	62 - 46

 Time: Score: /32

Triple Digit Subtraction

895 - 552	903 - 469	388 - 371	438 - 252
301 - 137	304 - 108	894 - 493	152 - 106
851 - 146	537 - 447	530 - 311	853 - 159
682 - 311	169 - 166	689 - 643	288 - 177
477 - 368	500 - 487	995 - 366	824 - 150
970 - 792	935 - 235	536 - 332	904 - 363
204 - 150	880 - 341	834 - 542	966 - 830
907 - 364	148 - 118	936 - 526	986 - 660

 Time: Score: /32

907 - 460	974 - 805	985 - 368	596 - 527
547 - 262	597 - 432	848 - 115	818 - 794
211 - 152	525 - 174	757 - 567	724 - 465
978 - 319	539 - 235	415 - 229	328 - 145
861 - 221	649 - 619	964 - 813	446 - 213
531 - 462	975 - 114	961 - 457	925 - 621
716 - 713	911 - 210	376 - 114	522 - 477
977 - 567	731 - 277	728 - 299	915 - 102

Time: Score: /32

Triple Digit Subtraction

866 - 494	763 - 457	855 - 612	704 - 624
830 - 636	959 - 501	702 - 367	220 - 150
268 - 196	611 - 184	425 - 392	763 - 619
801 - 170	869 - 465	849 - 613	952 - 474
456 - 386	738 - 281	336 - 133	856 - 333
777 - 328	670 - 141	560 - 132	954 - 173
390 - 374	848 - 618	894 - 215	888 - 618
962 - 714	382 - 132	324 - 205	875 - 649

Notes

Time: Score: /32

719 - 214	896 - 495	984 - 577	799 - 743
609 - 543	891 - 674	655 - 447	970 - 399
687 - 399	837 - 806	705 - 414	799 - 197
968 - 552	669 - 582	458 - 405	527 - 498
751 - 107	923 - 226	204 - 164	611 - 380
759 - 445	782 - 598	645 - 353	952 - 725
958 - 348	917 - 577	791 - 160	235 - 148
561 - 524	784 - 433	765 - 329	827 - 459

 Notes

 Time: Score: /32

Triple Digit Subtraction

371 - 106	535 - 387	326 - 131	975 - 532
811 - 510	440 - 321	868 - 165	985 - 721
385 - 108	902 - 344	923 - 287	879 - 441
977 - 430	723 - 183	849 - 308	383 - 352
772 - 674	966 - 270	995 - 729	948 - 281
772 - 219	818 - 198	583 - 525	663 - 642
980 - 222	663 - 401	918 - 423	845 - 162
604 - 516	749 - 681	644 - 205	700 - 311

 Time:

Score: /32

629 - 359	577 - 164	849 - 215	274 - 218
914 - 211	817 - 107	612 - 143	790 - 363
868 - 119	997 - 953	894 - 557	745 - 341
431 - 102	381 - 296	321 - 251	925 - 695
986 - 248	541 - 281	716 - 406	424 - 130
587 - 403	760 - 557	911 - 339	640 - 276
961 - 776	975 - 777	512 - 495	565 - 249
933 - 220	831 - 274	599 - 216	542 - 310

Notes

Time: **Score:**   /32

817 - 645	987 - 976	772 - 737	565 - 298
446 - 241	786 - 481	993 - 900	733 - 129
825 - 707	719 - 619	243 - 149	812 - 370
748 - 439	955 - 300	839 - 768	799 - 502
942 - 338	822 - 713	546 - 303	938 - 347
996 - 663	845 - 741	965 - 101	875 - 430
779 - 768	875 - 118	858 - 704	830 - 514
841 - 520	598 - 210	724 - 447	468 - 301

Notes

 Time:

Score:

 /32

356 - 114	641 - 320	671 - 390	789 - 680
582 - 363	898 - 539	817 - 120	126 - 102
766 - 685	976 - 564	759 - 661	941 - 930
937 - 137	943 - 889	582 - 529	813 - 691
643 - 289	350 - 166	452 - 364	992 - 686
993 - 370	753 - 696	965 - 615	662 - 421
659 - 368	616 - 353	878 - 109	841 - 182
567 - 135	808 - 490	595 - 178	720 - 273

 Time: Score: /32

Triple Digit Subtraction

414 - 165	890 - 466	568 - 551	867 - 333
820 - 681	366 - 176	637 - 198	344 - 245
836 - 484	725 - 342	552 - 468	821 - 372
861 - 484	650 - 167	558 - 545	451 - 244
987 - 477	983 - 724	722 - 113	693 - 382
533 - 421	919 - 548	982 - 867	802 - 634
832 - 599	182 - 122	501 - 297	782 - 632
920 - 391	984 - 752	745 - 286	551 - 508

Notes

Time: Score: /32

984 - 577	740 - 709	190 - 143	815 - 241
947 - 905	900 - 402	552 - 461	959 - 621
851 - 718	389 - 363	923 - 784	815 - 758
785 - 740	413 - 381	899 - 124	875 - 343
791 - 748	834 - 588	869 - 316	865 - 820
950 - 277	570 - 392	733 - 100	959 - 857
161 - 140	767 - 372	672 - 260	558 - 317
795 - 723	807 - 505	898 - 309	896 - 544

Notes

 Time: **Score:**   /**32**

471 - 126	852 - 245	379 - 126	790 - 671
784 - 114	829 - 555	906 - 560	524 - 163
918 - 129	667 - 165	995 - 420	793 - 217
794 - 690	539 - 139	792 - 343	668 - 106
568 - 293	372 - 216	942 - 171	338 - 262
611 - 149	149 - 103	748 - 741	454 - 350
557 - 350	597 - 489	928 - 427	942 - 548
906 - 671	962 - 839	619 - 313	715 - 471

Notes

 Time: **Score:** /32

482 - 381	826 - 198	773 - 698	303 - 270
594 - 202	473 - 296	381 - 342	891 - 716
361 - 338	783 - 308	812 - 773	171 - 109
557 - 454	996 - 427	333 - 327	558 - 475
641 - 324	763 - 539	501 - 472	770 - 542
455 - 286	380 - 264	813 - 430	995 - 454
857 - 620	850 - 546	908 - 452	727 - 653
983 - 953	714 - 601	884 - 813	739 - 595

Time: Score: /32

844 - 304	878 - 421	868 - 407	786 - 759
827 - 149	888 - 380	528 - 371	996 - 824
484 - 360	945 - 158	596 - 306	259 - 198
993 - 985	944 - 505	967 - 694	655 - 132
521 - 388	755 - 373	490 - 245	974 - 157
998 - 345	597 - 593	278 - 100	201 - 195
530 - 138	821 - 422	400 - 99	545 - 424
729 - 280	643 - 569	484 - 284	670 - 177

 Time: Score: /32

Triple Digit Subtraction

835 - 268	684 - 316	858 - 501	189 - 115
997 - 461	935 - 824	842 - 446	656 - 324
601 - 366	648 - 600	761 - 732	452 - 353
560 - 493	396 - 377	903 - 714	519 - 346
728 - 258	852 - 572	992 - 273	693 - 575
991 - 689	707 - 326	921 - 815	455 - 147
946 - 593	819 - 640	833 - 426	819 - 752
881 - 554	901 - 283	729 - 161	838 - 420

Notes

Time: **Score:** /**32**

620 - 332	868 - 557	778 - 534	451 - 312
974 - 175	782 - 524	977 - 727	798 - 448
953 - 541	951 - 480	697 - 365	760 - 264
534 - 532	686 - 396	400 - 169	633 - 320
279 - 185	801 - 715	982 - 643	567 - 221
843 - 115	595 - 116	715 - 478	543 - 467
622 - 541	858 - 317	881 - 773	942 - 860
806 - 461	901 - 120	900 - 511	644 - 394

 Time: Score: /32

Triple Digit Subtraction

664 - 309	864 - 151	624 - 329	799 - 340
713 - 459	404 - 178	636 - 611	752 - 111
285 - 175	461 - 327	191 - 184	664 - 584
688 - 558	532 - 219	925 - 207	988 - 346
812 - 308	557 - 165	885 - 737	645 - 490
771 - 236	914 - 657	996 - 899	535 - 266
942 - 122	899 - 677	823 - 456	744 - 253
619 - 408	553 - 537	794 - 588	457 - 133

Notes

Time: Score: /32

913 - 166	835 - 820	841 - 613	651 - 277
843 - 424	214 - 179	649 - 533	698 - 436
764 - 435	940 - 157	539 - 127	522 - 176
982 - 487	758 - 640	512 - 467	472 - 185
143 - 124	302 - 299	562 - 281	434 - 340
677 - 425	734 - 537	658 - 275	466 - 402
652 - 375	895 - 227	836 - 691	730 - 230
953 - 884	661 - 310	426 - 255	497 - 111

 Time: Score: /32

Triple Digit Subtraction

696 - 555	898 - 288	397 - 351	811 - 533
934 - 131	650 - 368	454 - 248	969 - 697
235 - 134	693 - 238	997 - 273	949 - 285
722 - 324	792 - 763	770 - 602	958 - 125
749 - 599	830 - 790	671 - 586	936 - 600
703 - 546	839 - 634	742 - 359	998 - 687
871 - 515	964 - 716	988 - 595	848 - 638
758 - 464	127 - 121	760 - 526	514 - 312

Notes

_____

_____

_____

_____

_____

 Time: Score: /32

999 - 217	830 - 827	153 - 126	521 - 405
707 - 276	700 - 437	527 - 170	600 - 460
777 - 479	600 - 322	443 - 254	552 - 201
700 - 451	797 - 291	933 - 503	744 - 562
759 - 106	603 - 275	949 - 498	834 - 427
520 - 245	961 - 276	714 - 127	566 - 176
668 - 377	787 - 657	383 - 304	971 - 276
326 - 154	930 - 321	506 - 262	943 - 162

 Time: Score:

Double Digit Multiplication

644 x 58	457 x 42	394 x 85	459 x 38
662 x 85	593 x 80	314 x 85	673 x 57
973 x 80	434 x 83	905 x 62	712 x 45
682 x 49	971 x 17	443 x 76	740 x 17
751 x 32	266 x 34	642 x 91	733 x 78
728 x 96	360 x 34	760 x 71	217 x 70

Time: Score: /24

Double Digit Multiplication

262 x 82	671 x 49	104 x 62	967 x 84
297 x 73	562 x 16	486 x 57	230 x 46
994 x 96	209 x 42	214 x 24	127 x 39
782 x 55	582 x 16	557 x 63	255 x 70
708 x 96	816 x 52	820 x 69	182 x 36
520 x 82	404 x 71	793 x 73	975 x 49

 Time: Score: /24

Double Digit Multiplication

763 x 79	894 x 10	113 x 22	779 x 78
584 x 48	463 x 28	893 x 72	817 x 13
460 x 90	692 x 54	313 x 47	357 x 61
168 x 11	299 x 25	948 x 57	849 x 40
269 x 19	239 x 63	544 x 66	612 x 78
632 x 92	110 x 55	784 x 42	841 x 30

Time: Score: /24

Double Digit Multiplication

634 x 75	155 x 13	964 x 95	275 x 88
710 x 97	177 x 95	130 x 64	853 x 44
964 x 93	936 x 62	153 x 53	753 x 27
508 x 22	646 x 83	664 x 31	792 x 15
841 x 49	673 x 68	800 x 19	569 x 78
503 x 98	620 x 84	661 x 79	586 x 70

 Time: **Score:**   /**24**

Double Digit Multiplication

880 x 92	463 x 79	676 x 86	862 x 47
870 x 9	634 x 60	524 x 36	312 x 12
654 x 77	563 x 91	305 x 36	526 x 40
333 x 32	99 x 59	690 x 31	105 x 64
219 x 22	132 x 74	469 x 20	363 x 87
511 x 28	329 x 38	919 x 89	189 x 65

Time: Score: /24

Double Digit Multiplication

579 x 75	316 x 85	403 x 77	241 x 29
563 x 95	899 x 58	381 x 67	667 x 30
475 x 55	953 x 37	877 x 87	669 x 86
152 x 67	820 x 69	359 x 96	499 x 15
949 x 44	594 x 29	417 x 12	745 x 86
317 x 51	911 x 47	665 x 74	583 x 20

 Time: **Score:**   /**24**

Double Digit Multiplication

179 x 34	333 x 91	414 x 35	336 x 60
747 x 51	828 x 95	120 x 15	595 x 45
478 x 73	756 x 36	212 x 49	917 x 15
584 x 72	250 x 33	473 x 37	208 x 10
279 x 33	196 x 30	639 x 82	816 x 53
664 x 59	807 x 35	201 x 16	860 x 48

Time: Score: /24

Double Digit Multiplication

369 x 95	582 x 25	299 x 92	166 x 73
360 x 51	683 x 29	980 x 39	606 x 67
130 x 52	716 x 43	380 x 16	842 x 70
971 x 94	713 x 30	299 x 82	515 x 61
554 x 34	197 x 39	484 x 76	874 x 43
354 x 82	217 x 38	228 x 89	947 x 54

Time: Score: /24

Double Digit Multiplication

591 x 16	156 x 32	397 x 64	429 x 94
696 x 68	770 x 31	683 x 30	796 x 9
399 x 81	187 x 90	120 x 58	213 x 39
765 x 97	376 x 48	245 x 42	711 x 48
731 x 12	458 x 9	165 x 92	144 x 94
839 x 45	804 x 89	993 x 73	220 x 35

Time: Score: /24

832 x 98	604 x 69	448 x 86	428 x 33
854 x 56	448 x 36	148 x 62	495 x 75
789 x 31	257 x 48	351 x 73	971 x 96
493 x 30	275 x 70	956 x 76	779 x 15
892 x 74	760 x 20	905 x 19	507 x 99
656 x 35	709 x 72	555 x 38	995 x 18

 Time: **Score:**   **/24**

Double Digit Multiplication

589 x 38	174 x 34	527 x 67	277 x 58
970 x 95	103 x 67	492 x 22	684 x 14
959 x 78	753 x 43	399 x 25	673 x 9
862 x 17	778 x 32	264 x 62	285 x 75
903 x 86	523 x 15	796 x 19	131 x 59
744 x 17	843 x 72	475 x 71	525 x 32

Time:　　　　Score:　　　/24

Double Digit Multiplication

711 x 89	950 x 66	705 x 47	417 x 11
977 x 18	731 x 56	935 x 95	258 x 86
436 x 37	348 x 19	313 x 95	997 x 24
775 x 79	189 x 42	669 x 32	315 x 73
956 x 9	604 x 70	941 x 44	209 x 19
533 x 17	500 x 47	493 x 28	637 x 78

 Time: Score: /24

Double Digit Multiplication

131 x 48	419 x 28	658 x 99	345 x 72
479 x 15	440 x 56	575 x 31	729 x 41
920 x 36	137 x 77	746 x 81	518 x 83
551 x 42	541 x 91	668 x 41	989 x 80
401 x 31	507 x 69	576 x 72	284 x 53
707 x 49	320 x 87	491 x 36	772 x 38

Time: Score: /24

Double Digit Multiplication

701 x 31	815 x 29	909 x 83	746 x 74
953 x 44	962 x 78	408 x 96	143 x 55
682 x 87	560 x 88	647 x 99	811 x 61
647 x 42	116 x 24	760 x 15	763 x 22
231 x 53	167 x 56	383 x 15	863 x 68
665 x 62	236 x 9	725 x 47	470 x 35

 **Time:**   **Score:**   /24

Double Digit Multiplication

104 x 18	894 x 55	108 x 79	552 x 95
476 x 50	117 x 68	416 x 10	868 x 45
109 x 18	666 x 97	513 x 50	791 x 32
146 x 80	105 x 74	418 x 96	790 x 78
322 x 62	306 x 80	892 x 57	738 x 82
436 x 91	864 x 30	772 x 85	712 x 92

Time: Score: /24

Double Digit Division

31 | 7798

95 | 4338

51 | 1930

93 | 2785

35 | 9434

77 | 9295

23 | 3548

24 | 8988

67 | 5864

63 | 3498

34 | 8695

75 | 7153

 Time:

Score: /12

Double Digit Division

83 | 1428

75 | 9089

27 | 5759

70 | 6207

51 | 5012

57 | 4169

73 | 2657

67 | 3255

74 | 5924

47 | 3460

33 | 8783

28 | 9983

Notes

 Time:

Score: /12

Double Digit Division

59 | 7343

49 | 8393

86 | 2985

15 | 5527

53 | 5979

37 | 6517

20 | 7310

25 | 8103

65 | 5278

21 | 1514

66 | 7458

35 | 1545

Notes

Time:

Score:

/12

Double Digit Division

35 | 2093   44 | 7685   78 | 1782

76 | 2001   26 | 3600   97 | 6251

62 | 1840   15 | 8707   60 | 1877

25 | 1757   23 | 6104   15 | 9989

 Time: Score: /12

60 | 2582

69 | 7847

83 | 6093

13 | 7033

79 | 1779

81 | 6554

47 | 3793

62 | 5464

53 | 5513

42 | 9119

40 | 1106

69 | 2523

Notes

 Time:

Score: /12

Double Digit Division

23 | 7296

26 | 7918

42 | 9796

14 | 1916

28 | 8811

57 | 9521

87 | 9522

89 | 5651

18 | 5209

60 | 1781

87 | 7738

79 | 9762

Time:

Score: /12

Double Digit Division

18 | 2664   72 | 1993   79 | 3268

37 | 5192   51 | 6739   58 | 6653

38 | 6782   56 | 6926   86 | 8540

31 | 3078   38 | 9060   33 | 6613

 Time: **Score:**   /**12**

Double Digit Division

82 | 6511   43 | 8329   49 | 5566

50 | 6984   78 | 9697   52 | 6559

21 | 2619   72 | 1963   65 | 2426

82 | 9765   63 | 2662   88 | 6972

 Time: Score: /12

Double Digit Division

44 | 2603   52 | 9837   32 | 4233

32 | 8127   78 | 9788   64 | 8786

82 | 2382   66 | 5705   82 | 6302

31 | 1248   26 | 1389   56 | 4955

 Time: Score:

Double Digit Division

80 | 7380

42 | 4828

87 | 6276

73 | 3049

61 | 2401

78 | 4787

56 | 5641

54 | 6526

79 | 9939

25 | 8074

91 | 1937

25 | 7423

 Time: Score: /12

Double Digit Division

51 | 5445

25 | 7236

84 | 6685

20 | 9506

40 | 4865

49 | 1341

74 | 3837

13 | 4524

73 | 4077

64 | 9285

34 | 8136

54 | 1800

 Time:

Score:

 12

68 | 6764   26 | 5271   97 | 7197

49 | 5320   13 | 9053   68 | 8920

34 | 9904   55 | 1720   55 | 1650

47 | 7201   96 | 5358   79 | 1778

 Time: Score: /12

55 | 6564

87 | 6961

43 | 4710

81 | 6226

91 | 7320

66 | 8093

81 | 3817

51 | 7624

56 | 9591

91 | 4150

31 | 4069

35 | 2289

 Time:

Score: /12

Double Digit Division

38 | 7639

14 | 4886

70 | 5573

94 | 5590

23 | 3353

70 | 7403

82 | 3364

24 | 8430

17 | 1667

22 | 9665

51 | 2742

96 | 1329

 Time: **Score:**   /**12**

59 | 9786

76 | 8441

40 | 6920

17 | 9847

80 | 1661

80 | 3291

41 | 1123

94 | 6422

15 | 9005

65 | 4396

30 | 3856

63 | 3777

 Time:

Score:

 /12

Made in the USA
Columbia, SC
25 October 2024